Warriors

Terry Deary

Illustrated by Mike Phillips

Scholastic Children's Books,
Euston House, 24 Eversholt Street,
London, NW1 1DB, UK

A division of Scholastic Ltd
London ~ New York ~ Toronto ~ Sydney ~ Auckland
Mexico City ~ New Delhi ~ Hong Kong

First published in the UK by Scholastic Ltd, 2007

10 digit ISBN 0 439 94330 2
13 digit ISBN 978 0439 94330 7

Printed and bound by Tien Wah Press Pte. Ltd, Malaysia

2 4 6 8 10 9 7 5 3 1

Contents

Introduction

Some people enjoy fighting. People like boxers, wrestlers and footballers. People like the school bully...

But in history there have been millions of people who like fighting so much they make it their job. Warriors...

And when warriors fight, they often fight to kill.

Why do they behave like that? They are human beings, like you, yet they are ten times more violent. They have some disgusting stories to tell.

You really ought to hear those stories. Behind the shields and armour, the helmets and weapons there are real people.

Learn about warriors in history and you may learn a bit about the bullies in your own world. Learn about bullies and you may learn how to stop them!

Mind you, not every bully in history has been beaten by kindness. In ancient times, the Philistines had thousands of soldiers. But they had one super-soldier ... giant warrior Goliath.

The Philistines thought he was an unbeatable big bully. Yet he was brought down by a boy ... David.

David's greatest weapon was his wits!

Yes, all right. David won with wits AND his skill with weapons. To find out more about how history's super-soldier won – and lost – you need a horrible history of warriors. Where will you find one of those?

Awful Egyptians

Ancient warriors who bashed their way to victory
Place: Egypt, Africa. Time: 3000–300 BC

The Egyptians settled on the banks of the Nile and became rich. Of course other nations wanted their riches and attacked them.

Egypt had problems with invasions from bandits (who wanted to pinch their cattle), from tribes like 'The Sea People' who had lost their own land, and from other nations like the Hittites who wanted the power and wealth of Egypt.

The pharaohs needed armies. An Egyptian schoolbook says an Egyptian soldier's life was tough.

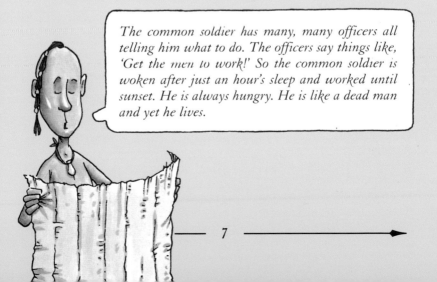

The common soldier has many, many officers all telling him what to do. The officers say things like, 'Get the men to work!' So the common soldier is woken after just an hour's sleep and worked until sunset. He is always hungry. He is like a dead man and yet he lives.

A bit like going to school today, isn't it?
What do you know about them? Try this tricky test.
Which is the odd one out in these groups?

① A SOLDIER'S WEAPONS WERE... A STONE-HEADED CLUB, A SPEAR, A BRONZE AXE, A POISON DART BLOWER

I NEED MORE ARMS!

② A COMMON SOLDIER PROTECTED HIMSELF WITH... A SHIELD, A MOP OF THICK HAIR, A HELMET, A LINEN APRON

OOPS!

③ WHEN THE ARMY WASN'T AT WAR THE SOLDIERS HAD OTHER TASKS... POLICEMEN, PALACE GUARDS, FIREMEN, MESSENGERS

④ A SOLDIER'S CHARIOT HAD...TYRES, WEAPON-RACKS, DOORS, TWO HORSES

WHERE'S THE START BUTTON?

⑤ AN EGYPTIAN ARMY TRAVELLED WITH...LAUNDRY WOMEN, WEAPON-MAKERS, COOKS, WRITERS

Answers:

The odd ones out are:

1) A poison dart blower. The main weapon was the club (known today as a 'mace') to beat out your enemy's brains.

2) A helmet. Only the officers had helmets. The ordinary soldiers grew their hair thick to take the club blows and wore aprons to protect their naughty bits. They didn't even wear shoes.

3) Firemen. The Egyptians had a good messenger service and soldiers took news from fortress to fortress so the pharaoh always knew what was happening. These forts were about 80 kilometres apart. They also used soldiers as a police force and of course to parade as the pharaoh's guardsmen.

4) Doors. The Egyptians learned from Asia how to use horses but never rode them in battle, only used them to pull chariots. Their chariots usually carried a driver and a warrior. The floor was made of woven leather because a solid floor would have given a bouncy, travel-sick-making ride. The wheels had leather tyres to hold them together. (They didn't have strong glue and screws in those days!)

5) Laundry women. As the soldiers only wore loincloths they didn't need anyone to do their washing for them, but they did take an army of cooks and weapon-makers and porters to carry their food and beer.

Gruesome Goths

Fierce fighters who brought blood to Europe

Place: Eastern Europe. Time: 1st century–8th century AD

The Goths smashed the Romans at Adrianople in AD 378. They had some nasty habits.

They had been driven from their homes by the Huns from the East. They were so desperate they traded with the Romans ... some families would swap one of their kids for a dog. Why?

Would your dad swap you for a dog so he could eat the dog for dinner?

The Goths decided to fight the Romans when the Romans let them starve.

The Romans thought the Goth warriors could be chicken at times. When the Romans fired a huge boulder at them ... and missed ... the Goths were scared.

Then when the Goths marched to Constantinople they met a Saracen group fighting with the Romans.

One Saracen rode into the middle of the Goth warriors. He was wearing just a loincloth and screaming war cries...

He slashed the throat of one Goth and drank the blood.

The Goths gave up and went off to find somebody easier to fight.

Cut-throat Celts

Powerful people with a horrible taste for heads
Place: Northern Europe. Time: Dark Ages (around AD 476–1000)

The Celts were fierce fighters. Some of the stories about Celtic warriors were reported by the Roman historians, so they are usually believed. In fact the Romans may have exaggerated a bit to make their own soldiers look better.

Here are ten cut-throat Celt facts you probably didn't want to know…

1 Irish Celt warrior Cu Chulainn went mad in battle. He became so full of blood lust that he couldn't tell friend from enemy.

2 The early Celtic warriors fought with no clothes on, except perhaps a gold band around the neck called a torque. They didn't believe in wearing armour. The Celts knew their gods would decide if they were to die that day. All the armour in the world wouldn't protect them. The Romans were protected by armour … and underpants!

3 The Celts were very bad losers. If they looked like losing they would kill themselves. In one cheerful Roman statue a Celtic warrior is shown plunging a sword into his chest with one hand while holding his dead wife in the other. He has already

killed her to save her from capture. Hope she was grateful!

4 The crafty Celts were great riders and used a special saddle for fighting. They had no stirrups for their feet so they were always in danger of falling off their horses. The Celtic saddle of the second and third centuries BC had four high bumps (pommels is the posh word) that a warrior could grip with his legs. That left one hand free to guide the horse and one to hold a weapon.

5 In AD 52 an army of 50,000 Romans defeated 250,000 Celtic Gauls led by Vercingetorix. The trouble was the Celts ran wild in battle and fought as individuals. The Romans worked as a team and won. (But the Roman historian may have been fibbing about the numbers.)

6 The Celts liked fighting so much they didn't just fight against enemies … they fought against each other! Celt tribe against Celt tribe. They also had a bit of fun fighting for other people as far away as Egypt, Greece and Asia Minor.

7 The Romans were really shocked by rebel British leader Queen Boudica. When Big Boud's husband died he left his land to Emperor Nero and Boud's daughters. The Emperor wanted it all and had Boudica and the daughters flogged. Big Bad Boud attacked Roman towns and was especially cruel to women prisoners. They were executed and bits of their bodies were cut off and stuck in their mouths. They then had sharp wooden stakes pushed through their bodies and they were hoisted up for everyone to see.

8 A Celtic chieftain's helmet found in Ciumesti in Romania has a large model raven perched on top. Ravens were seen as birds of war because they liked to hop down on to battlefields and chew on the corpses. The Ciumesti raven's wings are spread and are hinged in the middle so they can flap up and down! Historians believe the chieftain would only wear it on important occasions – not in battle.

9 There is no doubt that the ancient Celts believed that the greatest prize in battle was an enemy's head. They decorated their saddles with heads and they decorated the doors of their houses with heads. They kept old heads fresh in cedar oil and brought them out every now and again to boast about them. 'Here's one I killed earlier!'

10 The Celts believed that single combat was a good way to show off your bravery and settle an argument. Two heroes would step forward and begin by insulting each other!

Then they would start fighting while the soldiers on both sides watched to see that they fought fairly.

Heledd's savage song

Warriors were popular with poets. There are many poems about wars and heroes.

The Welsh wrote poems to remember their dead Celtic warriors ... even losers like Cynddylan who died in AD 656. This bloodthirsty poem is said to have been written by Cynddylan's sister, Heledd. In English it may sound a bit like this...

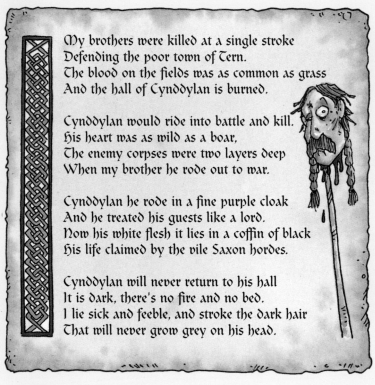

> My brothers were killed at a single stroke
> Defending the poor town of Tern.
> The blood on the fields was as common as grass
> And the hall of Cynddylan is burned.
>
> Cynddylan would ride into battle and kill.
> His heart was as wild as a boar,
> The enemy corpses were two layers deep
> When my brother he rode out to war.
>
> Cynddylan he rode in a fine purple cloak
> And he treated his guests like a lord.
> Now his white flesh it lies in a coffin of black
> His life claimed by the vile Saxon hordes.
>
> Cynddylan will never return to his hall
> It is dark, there's no fire and no bed.
> I lie sick and feeble, and stroke the dark hair
> That will never grow grey on his head.

Cheerful stuff, eh?

Horrible Huns

Horrible horsemen and hated hooligans

Place: Northern Asia and Europe. Time: Roman age and Dark Ages (around AD 376–500)

No one knows exactly where these fierce horse warriors came from ... the borders of China probably. But the Roman Empire knew when they arrived! From around AD 400 they rampaged round Europe.

Their greatest leader was Attila the Hun – an incredible man who was just 140 cm small.

Attila's Huns were not very popular. The Roman writer Ammianus Marcellinus made them sound like the worst football hooligans you ever met. He said...

> *The nation of the Huns are the worst of all Barbarians in wildness of life. And though they do just about look like men they are so backward that they make no use of fire. They use no spices when they prepare their food, but eat roots which they find in the fields. They also eat half-raw flesh of any sort of animal. I say half-raw, because they give it a kind of cooking by placing it between their own thighs and the backs of their horses.*

Pop down to your local Pony Club and try a thigh-fried chicken. Scrummy.

Nasty at Naissus

Around AD 440 Attila the Hun's men flattened the city of Naissus (in Serbia and Montenegro). The riverbank was so choked with corpses that the smell stopped people returning to the city for years after.

DID YOU KNOW...?

The Roman historian Ammianus Marcellinus said the Hun warriors made their cloaks from the skins of mice! (It would have taken hundreds of herds of mice if the Hun was fat.) But mutt-headed Marce got it WRONG. He was just repeating silly gossip. Don't believe everything you read – unless it's in a *Horrible Histories* book, of course.

Warrior wisdom

Attila the Hun had his ideas about warriors written down. Here are some you need to know if you ever decide to become a warrior...

1. A wise chief never kills the Hun bearing bad news. The wise chief kills the Hun who forgets to deliver bad news.

2. Warriors only make enemies on purpose.

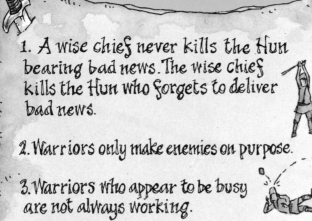

3. Warriors who appear to be busy are not always working.

4. Whatever you do there will be a risk.

5. Always watch your back.

6. Every warrior makes his own success. No other warrior can do it for him.

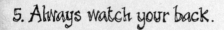

7. A warrior can get anything if he is willing to pay the price.

8. Written reports are only useful if they are read by the chief.

9. Every warrior has value - even if only to serve as a bad example.

10. Great chiefs never take themselves too seriously.

The warrior wants a wife

In AD 451 Attila the Hun was looking for a wife. He fell in love with the holy St Ursula. She turned him down. How did he take it?

He killed her with an arrow and had 11,000 of her followers massacred.

Attila found a wife in the end. But on the night of his wedding he got a nosebleed and bled to death.

What happened to his wife? Who nose?

DID YOU KNOW ...?

The Huns used to cut the faces of their sons when they became teenagers. The scars made them look tough and scary when they went to war.

Vicious Vikings

Nasty Norsemen who mashed monks

Place: Northern Europe. Time: Dark Ages (around AD 476–1000)

The Vikings lived in Norway, Denmark and Sweden. They were farmers and fishermen.

Then they became warriors. They left their homelands to raid the British Isles and Europe. They made brilliant ships and even sailed as far as America and Italy.

They often attacked helpless monks and stole their church treasures. But when they came up against a tough warrior like King Harold of England they had had their chips ... and their ships.

If there had been newspapers in 1066 the York headlines would have made rotten reading ...

YORK SUN
Wednesday 20 September 1066

Hooray for Hardrada!

This evening the Viking leader Hardrada is top man in Yorkshire. His nice Norwegian army smashed the English earls at Fulford this afternoon and I was there to see it.

The English held the high ground while Hardrada defended a ditch by the river. The English couldn't be beaten if they stayed up there.

But the valiant Viking Hardrada had a perfect plan – he sent out a weak force to defend the eastern end of the ditch. The English thought they would win easily so they left the hill and attacked. When they were in the ditch Hardrada struck.

The ditch had been damp at the start of the day. Soon it was deep in English blood. The battlefield had been marshy but the Vikings now kept their feet dry – they simply used the English corpses, like stepping-stones.

Tired but happy, Hardrada told me, 'I do not plan to enter the city of York. I do not want it looted. I will take hostages from the city. If the English try to attack again I will massacre the hostages!'

And the victorious Viking means it. I know, I am one of the hostages. York has also delivered 150 children to the Norsemen. So let's welcome our Viking victors!

OUR REPORTER- HAPPY TO GREET HARDRADA

Hardrada had beaten the northern army, but King Harold arrived with an army from the south and caught the Vikings napping ... yes, really!

The Vikings were dozing in the sun at Stamford Bridge – 10 miles (16 km) from Fulford. Harold attacked before most Vikings could get their weapons or armour on.

After a bitter battle Harold won. The reporter would have had a different story on that day!

YORK ☀ SUN

Monday 25 September 1066

Hero Harold hammers horrible Hardrada

The vicious Vikings have been vanquished! And the folk of York say good riddance to the ruthless raiders! Here today, at Stamford Bridge, hopeless Hardrada died with thousands of his awful army when our king's awesome army nobbled the Norse nasties

There are two famous stories about the battle that everyone should know…

1 A lone Viking warrior blocked a bridge to stop the English crossing, giving his friends time to gather some weapons. He killed some of the English before they killed him with a trick. They sent a boat under the bridge, pushed a pike through the planks and stabbed him from below.

NOW *THAT'S* BELOW THE BELT!

2 Harold offered part of his kingdom to one of the raiders – his brother Tostig. But Tostig wanted land for Hardrada too. Harold answered…

> *I will give him just seven feet of English land – enough to bury him.*

And Harold kept his word. Hardrada died with an arrow in the throat. Tostig was hacked to death when he refused to surrender.

Slay that servant

The Vikings buried their greatest warriors in their longships.

A longship grave was dug up in 1880 at Oseberg (Norway). Inside there were two WOMEN.

One must have been the wife of a posh warrior. The other was probably her slave … still slaving away in the afterlife.

But that slave would have been alive at the time the posh woman died. The Vikings must have murdered the serving girl.

There were also ten horses slaughtered and buried in the same grave.

NEIGH, BUT THAT'S NASTY

Warrior women

Warriors in history have mostly been men. But sometimes women have gone to war and taught the men a thing or two. Here are ten things about warrior women they never tell you at school...

1 Amazing Amazons

The most famous women warriors were the Amazons from the Greek legends. In the *Iliad* the Amazons were referred to as *Antianneira* which means 'those that fight like men'. Maybe there was some truth in the tales. Maybe the stories were about the fighting Scythian women of around 500 BC.

Graves in Scythia show that the Scythians buried women's skeletons with bows, swords and horses.

2 Incredible Indians

The Rig Veda, an old poem of India written between 3500 and 1800 BC, tells the story of a warrior, Queen Vishpla. She lost her leg in a battle, was fitted with an iron leg and went back to the battle.

3 Cut-throat Celts

No one knows exactly where the Celts came from, but from central Europe they spread in all directions until they came up against the Romans. In 102 BC a Roman writer, Plutarch, described a battle against the Celts. He said…

> The fight was just as fierce with the women as with the men ... the women charged with swords and axes and fell upon their enemy giving a hideous cry.

Of course, the fiercest of all warrior Celts was Boudica. See page 14 for more about Big Bad Boud.

4 Gruesome Gauls

The Gauls lived in the place we now call France. Roman historian Ammianus Marcellinus said Gaulish wives were even stronger than their husbands.

> They fight with their fists and kick at the same time like stones from a catapult.

THIS IS ALL VERY GAULLING

5 Vicious Vikings

Some Viking women got bored with staying at home. They dressed as Viking warriors and fought.

At the battle of Bravellir three women (Hethna, Visna and Vebiorg) were captains in the army of King Harald War-tooth.

Rusilla fought against her brother Thrond for the thrones of Denmark and Norway.

As for Hervor, she learned to use bow, shield and sword. But how did she start out? In a battle? No, as a mugger.

Not all of the Viking warriors liked to see their women fighting. Auðr was divorced by her husband because she wore trousers like a man. She attacked him with a sword in revenge.

6 Savage Scots

Isobel, Countess of Buchan (1296–1358) left her husband, the Earl of Buchan, to fight with the Scottish rebel Bruce. She pinched hubby's best warhorses and took them with her.

Her husband sent out an order for her death but the English armies captured her first. Isobel was taken to England, shut in a small cage and hung over the walls of Berwick town for four years.

When she was released she went to a convent.

7 Duelling Dona

Dona Catalina de Erauso of San Sebastian LEFT a convent in 1596 and became a warrior.

She sailed to Peru to fight the Incas and make her fortune. She used a sword, a knife and a pistol.

But she didn't just fight in battles. She picked fights with other Spanish soldiers and fought duels.

She died around 1650.

8 Arc lass to ashes

Joan of Arc is the most famous woman warrior of all time.

In 1429 Joan led the French army and drove the English invaders away from Orléans. It was her first great victory. But in 1431 she was captured, put on trial, and burned by the English as a witch.

This peasant girl didn't fight against the French enemies because she enjoyed it, she did it because she believed God told her to.

People in those days were very superstitious. In Joan's local church there was a statue of a young Christian who died for his faith. It was said that the man was beheaded – then picked up his head and gave a sermon with it before he died.

If Joan believed that then she could believe God told her…

In 1452 Joan of Arc was put on trial again – without her being there. Not even her ashes. This time she was found not guilty! A bit late by then.

DID YOU KNOW…?

Burned bits of human are in a museum in Chinon. They include a rib and some skin. They are said to have been found at a stake in the Normandy town of Rouen, where Joan of Arc was burned in 1431.

On 14 February 2006 the museum said scientists were going to test the skin and bone to see if they really could belong to Joan.

9 Cruel Catherine

Catherine the Great (1729–96) led rebels in an attack on her husband Tsar Peter III of Russia (1728–62).

Peter liked to play with his toy soldiers, under the bedclothes, every night. He had tiny forts and cannon under there. Cute, eh? Cute for a 10-year-old boy – but Pete was 34 years old.

He ended up murdered. Catherine was blamed but she may not have had anything to do with Pete popping off. He was strangled.

Cruel Cath wore a soldier's uniform and directed the tactics of her wars up until 1796.

10 Mean Queen

Amina, Queen of Nigeria (died 1610), started fighting at the age of 16 to increase her empire.

Every time she captured a town she found herself a new boyfriend from that town. Lucky men? Not really. After one night she had the man beheaded next morning. A meaner Amina you cannot imagine!

HORRIBLE HISTORIES FOUL FACT

Even when women weren't being warriors they could still help their soldiers. In the English Civil War (1642–9) the troops needed lots of gunpowder.

An important part of gunpowder was saltpetre. This was made from bird-droppings and … human pee.

Roundhead officers had the right to dig these ingredients from hen-houses and toilets.

In 1638 'Saltpetre men' tried to get permission to go into churches to collect material because, they said…

Mangling Mongols

Horrors on hairy horses were hungry for power

Place: Mongolia. Time: Middle Ages

The Mongols were horse warriors. They almost lived on their horses – and when they got hungry they ate them.

If you are in the vast plains of Mongolia and there isn't a burger bar in sight, then how do you cook a horse? Here's one idea…

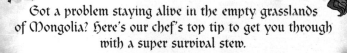

Survival stew

Got a problem staying alive in the empty grasslands of Mongolia? Here's our chef's top tip to get you through with a super survival stew.

+ First, catch a horse and kill it.
+ Now skin the horse carefully so you don't split the skin.
+ Gut the horse and throw away the guts.
+ Fill the skin with water. Light a fire and place large stones in the fire.
+ Place the hot stones in the water so it boils.
+ Put the horse flesh in the boiling water till it is cooked.

Eat and enjoy your tasty stew.

The Mongols had to cook in muddy water, but it gave them the strength to go out and conquer the world.

What did they do if they had no horses? The Mongols were starving at the siege of Beijing in 1214. Disease killed thousands of men. It was said they ate the corpses.

Genghis Khan (1162–1227)

Genghis grew up to lead the Mongol people to conquer a huge part of the world – he probably ruled a larger area than any other leader in history. And you don't do that by being nice to grannies and giving lollipops to kids.

In 1221 Khan headed towards Europe. The town of Merv stood in his way. The people fought, but the army of Genghis defeated them.

It was said Khan's men killed a million in a day – the worst day's massacre in history. It may have been as many as 1,300,000 unarmed men, women and children. Of course Genghis didn't kill them himself. Each Mongol soldier killed about three or four hundred helpless people that day.

On 18 August 1227 mighty Genghis died. We do know he was fighting the Tanguts at the time. The trouble is, no one is

quite sure HOW he died. Here are the three most popular ideas:

1 He was so old he fell off his horse and the fall killed him.
2 He went to war against the Tangut Empire and was killed.
3 He forced a Tangut princess to marry him. She hid a dagger in her clothes. As soon as they were alone together she sliced off his naughty bits and he bled to death ... he was too embarrassed to cry out for help!

Tamerlane the terror (1336–1405)

Tamerlane ruled the Mongols in the 1300s. His family said he would grow up to be a terror. How did they know? Because baby Tamerlane was born with blood-filled hands. A deadly sign.

Sure enough his hands were steeped in blood for the rest of his life.

When Tartar terror Tamerlane the Great invaded India he reached Delhi. He massacred 100,000 Hindu prisoners. Why?

Because it was too much trouble to feed them and guard them.

Then he entered the city and killed ANOTHER 100,000!

In 1383 he had 2,000 prisoners buried alive at Sabzawar.

Then he had 5,000 beheaded at Zirih and piled up their heads to make a pyramid.

HEADS WILL ROLL FOR THIS!

Worst cursed

Tamerlane was buried in Persia (now Uzbekistan).

A Russian scientist dug up the body on 19 June 1941. A curse carved on the tomb said...

Three days later, on 21 June 1941, Germany invaded Russia and millions of Russians died.

I bet Tamerlane's ghost was saying, 'I told you so!'

Horrible Horsemen

Stick a warrior on a horse and he is faster in attack and faster running away. He can chop and stab from a height and the horse's hooves are another weapon. Then, in really tough times, he can kill the horse and eat it.

WHAT HAPPENED TO YOUR HORSE?

I GOT PECKISH

The Hittites were using horses for war in 1400 BC and they have been used ever since.

There have been some horrible horsemen in history ... and some horrible times for horses.

Cuirassier

Even in the 1800s some warriors were still riding into battle wearing armour. It was often a metal plate on the chest and the back. The posh word for this armour is 'cuirass', so these riders were known as 'cuirassiers'.

The French cuirassiers of the 1800s carried straight swords, held out like a lance. They thought they were the knights of Napoleon's army and refused to carry pistols – too common, they said.

This was brave – but daft. A bullet would go straight through a cuirass.

Dragoon

These were French horse soldiers who weren't so fussy about using guns on horses. From the 1500s these riders with guns were known as 'dragoons'.

But WHY?

a) Because he had to kill a dragon to join the dragoons.

b) Because he used to pull a cart behind him with a little cannon – it would 'drag on' the back of his horse.

c) Because he carried a short musket known as a dragoon.

Answer: c) A dragoon was a musketeer on a horse and his musket was also called a dragoon. He didn't drag it behind him but carried it in a leather bucket by his saddle till he needed to use it. Maybe he should have been called a bucketeer?

A dragoon rode into battle but fought on foot.

Lancer

The idea of a man charging around with a lance should have disappeared when guns were invented, but in 1807 Polish warriors began fighting with lances again.

Even more amazing, 'lancer' groups of British soldiers were STILL trying to attack with lances in World War I (1914–18) where their enemies were firing machine guns at them.

On 30 March 1918 a German force was defending Moreuil Wood. Lancers from Lord Strathcona's horse regiment charged at the German machine guns.

They won! The days of the knight with a lance were finally over for the British, but they ended with a victory ... of course.

There was one last battle for the Lancers of Poland 21 years later. Hitler attacked Poland on 1 September 1939. The Poles were taken completely by surprise. Polish lancers on horseback were slaughtered as they bravely charged at the German tanks.

Spahi

These Turkish knights became part of the army around 1445. They rode with the Sultan as his bodyguard.

They also had another special job to do for him. What was it?
a) They collected his taxes for him.
b) They collected his winnings from the lottery.
c) They collected his stamps.

Answer: a) You may not want to pay your taxes but if you see a man riding towards you with a whacking great sword you may pay a bit quicker.

Name that nag

Some horses became almost as famous as their masters. Alexander the Great's horse was so wild it ate the flesh of anyone (except Alex) who tried to handle him.

But what was that savage stallion's name?

Can you fit the horse to the hero? If you need some coltish clues here are the names in the wrong order: Red Hare, Chetak, Old Baldy, Ebenezer, Marengo, Vic, Copenhagen, Bucephalus, Babieca, Incitatus

1 Alexander The Great is the only man who can ride _____.

2 Rana Pratap Singh was saved in a bloody battle at Haldighati in 1576 by his horse _____.

3 El Cid (1044–99) asked for his warhorse _____ to be buried with him.

4 Major General George G. Meade's horse, _____, has been wounded 14 times in the American Civil War (1861–65).

5 Roman Emperor Caligula (AD 12–41) has made his warhorse, _____, a consul.

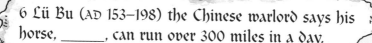

6 Lü Bu (AD 153–198) the Chinese warlord says his horse, _____, can run over 300 miles in a day.

7 Crowds gather in London to see Napoleon's famous warhorse, _____, after his defeat at Waterloo (1815).

8 THE DUKE OF WELLINGTON (1769–1852) RIDES IN TRIUMPH ON HIS HORSE _____

9 General Custer of the US Cavalry has been massacred by the Sioux Indians at the Little Big Horn River and his horse _____ died too.

10 Chief Joseph (1840-1904) of the Nez Perce tribe has the horse _____ that is famous for its speed.

Answers: 1) Bucephalus, 2) Chetak, 3) Babieca[1], 4) Old Baldy, 5) Incitatus, 6) Red Hare, 7) Marengo, 8) Copenhagen, 9) Vic, 10) Ebenezer

The last charge of Rattler

Corporal Dickson (1789–1880) was a Scottish horse soldier at the Battle of Waterloo when the British beat the French. He told what it was like for man and horse to be there. Dickson's horse was called Rattler and it somehow survived…

1 The name means 'Stupid' – neigh, it really does!

RATTLER'S LAST CHARGE

I dug my spur into my brave old Rattler, and we were off like the wind. Just then I saw Major Hankin fall wounded. I felt a strange thrill run through me, and I am sure my noble beast felt the same, for, after rearing for a moment, she sprang forward, uttering loud neighings and snortings, and leapt over the holly-hedge at a terrific speed.

It was a grand sight to see the long line of giant grey horses dashing along with flowing manes and heads down, tearing up the turf about them as they went. The men in their red coats and tall bearskins were cheering loudly, and the trumpeters were sounding the 'Charge'.

All of us were greatly excited, and began crying, 'Scotland for ever!' as we crossed the road. For we heard the Highland pipers playing among the smoke and firing below.

The French were fighting like tigers. Some of the
wounded were firing at us as we passed.

We had now reached the bottom of the slope.
There the ground was slippery with deep mud. The
ground was very soft so that our horses sank to the
knees as we struggled on. My brave Rattler was
becoming quite exhausted, but we dashed ever
onwards.

It was the last we saw of our colonel, poor fellow!
His body was found with both arms cut off. Major
Clarke said he saw him wounded, going at full
speed, and with the reins between his teeth, after he
had lost his hands.

Then we got among the guns, and we had our
revenge. Such slaughtering! Rattler lost her temper
and bit and tore at everything that came in her way.
She seemed to have got new strength. I never saw
horses become so fierce.

Around me there was just noise of clashing
arms, shouting of men, neighing and moaning of
horses. But my poor Rattler had lost much blood
from a lance-wound received in her last battle.

Sword-swishing samurai

Savage sword-swishers who severed several heads
Place: Japan. Time: 400s to 1800s

CHOP! CHOP!

These Japanese warriors used horses and armour in the 400s, long before the Normans and the knights of Europe came along.

Then, in AD 1192 Yoritomo became the first Shogun of Japan and set up his samurai knights as lords of the people.

They went on bossing Japan until the 1800s, long after 'knight' was just a title in Europe.

They were trained to be fearless and true to their lord, the Shogun.

At first they used bows and arrows with swords just for lopping off enemy heads. By the 1200s they started to use spears. They also spent more time fighting on foot, using two swords.

Now for the HORRIBLE history…

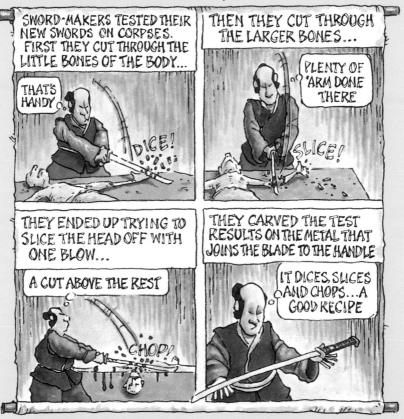

This test report would be a bit more interesting than your school test report of course.

You only get, 'Can do better' but samurai swords got 'Can cut butter'.

You get, 'Nice handwriting' but samurai swords got 'Nice hand-slicing'.

Now for the REALLY HORRIBLE history…

The swords would sometimes be tested on live criminals who were waiting to be executed. Instead of a fast finish they died a little bit at a time.

In AD 1876, Emperor Meiji made a new law that ended the wearing of swords. The samurai had lost their jobs – criminals kept their fingers and toes.

Kids get killed too

In 1185 at the Battle of Dan-no-ura, the samurai knights of Minamoto Yoritomo attacked the fleet of the Emperor of Japan. The Emperor was just six years old.

When the battle was lost the Emperor's granny threw him off the boat and drowned him to save him from Minamoto Yoritomo and his samurai.

Even today some Japanese believe the crabs hold the spirits of the dead warriors.

Poor crab!

HE'S BEEN TAKEN OVER BY A SAMURAI KNIGHT

HOW SHELLFISH!

☠ **DID YOU KNOW...?** ☠

If a samurai warrior was beaten on the battlefield he would kill himself rather than be captured. He would do 'hara-kiri', which means 'stomach-cutting'. He'd slice his guts and let them spill out. Sometimes he would be ordered to do this as a punishment, sometimes he would do it rather than be taken prisoner. Some samurai would die this way if their lord and leader died. You had to do the slicing without trembling or showing that it hurt. I could say, 'That took guts,' but you would NOT see such a dreadful joke in a *Horrible Histories* book, would you?

If you were really lucky a friend (or servant) would finish you off quickly with a chop to the neck.

Nasty ninja

Vanishing warriors vanquished very great numbers
Place: Japan. Time: 1500s

These were trained assassins from Asia. Their past is so secret even ninja warriors don't know it! But YOU will know if you're a ninja because you started training at the age of five.

You trained to be tough – like hanging from the branch of a tree for hours. That would HURT if you were just five years old!

The whole point about being a ninja is you were SNEAKY. Their main weapon was to be invisible – or at least not seen as an enemy.

In 1562 about 80 ninja attacked a castle in Kaminojo. They dressed as castle guards, which is a bit of a cheat. The other disguises they used were...

- Actor or musician – your flute has lead in it to make it a heavy club
- A homeless samurai – you can carry two swords
- A Buddhist monk – you hide weapons under those loose robes
- A trader – your walking cane hides a sharp blade

And ninja women were sent to flirt with the enemy – then pull a poison hairpin from their hair and stab him.

Ninjas would also use throwing stars (see page 49) to blind or injure an enemy. Sometimes they were poisoned and sometimes they were smeared in something that would make the victim ill if they were scratched. What?
a) deadly nightshade berry
b) ninja poo
c) school dinner stew

Answer: b) The ninja could use his own poo to make the throwing star even more deadly if you were scratched by it. The wound would be infected and kill you. Nasty knight. For a quicker kill the ninja could make cyanide poison from plums, cherries, apples, apricots and almonds, or use poisonous mushrooms or deadly blowfish poison.

☠ DID YOU KNOW...? ☠

Ninja warriors could tell the time without using a watch. They used the eyes of a cat, which changed at different times of the day as the light changed. Of course it would be easier just to ask a policeman.

Warrior weapons

Everyone knows about swords, bows and arrows, guns and spears, but warriors were always looking for new weapons to beat the old ones.

King Francis I of France (1494-1547) DIDN'T use the new weapons in battle against Italy and look what happened.

Francis believed that knights were gentlemen and should fight like gentlemen – on horses, with swords and lances. His army had guns but he wouldn't let them fire.

Francis and his knights charged at the Italian guns, waving their swords. Of course the Italians shot them down. Francis's horse was shot from under him and he was captured.

Six thousand French soldiers died – all because Francis wanted to fight like a gentleman.

Here are some weird warrior weapons you may not know about.

Pilum

This Roman spear had a sharp iron point held on with a bendy metal neck. The head bent when it hit your enemy's shield or his body. He couldn't pull it out so he couldn't throw it back at you! Dead enemies? Pilum up!

Shuriken

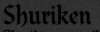

Shuriken means 'hand hidden blade' and they were used for throwing or stabbing. Handy! Poor ninja couldn't usually afford special weapons so they used ordinary objects from home. Shuriken were made from needles, nails, knives, coins and washers. They weren't usually deadly but they didn't half annoy the enemy.

Chakram

This Indian flat steel ring had a sharp edge and was thrown like a deadly doughnut, to cut off enemies' heads. Warriors would wear a turban with a point so they could carry several chakrams on their heads.

Ay-baita axe

A Turkish battle-axe; this had a
blade on one side and a pick on
the other so the warrior could
pick out the eyes of his enemy.
It had metal bands down the
wooden shaft for strength.

Fukumi-bari

These are tiny darts that Ninja
warriors kept hidden inside their
mouths. They rolled their tongues
into a tube and blew the fukumi-bari
into the eyes of their enemies.

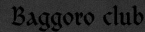

Baggoro club

If you haven't got metal then bag a baggoro. It's a flat club from Australia made of hardwood with a sharp edge.

Hora

An Indian weapon which was worn on the knuckles. This spiky weapon made of cow's horn meant you really made a point when you punched your enemy.

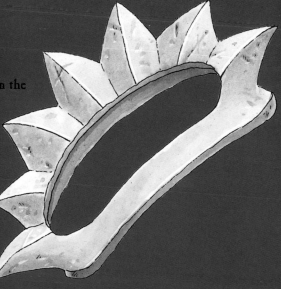

Tessen

A deadly fan – but not a football supporter ... a real fan. How cool is that? Samurai could take these folding fans to places where they couldn't sneak a sword. The edges were made of sharp iron. When they were folded they looked like normal fans. A tessen could also be used as a shield for pushing away arrows and darts. It could be thrown or even used to help a samurai swim – a sort of hand-flipper.

Patu

A short wooden club from the South Pacific – deadlier than a golf club. It could be made from bone or stone but best of all was the greenstone club. It could have shark teeth along the edge. Snappy. A prisoner of war might ask to be killed by the greenstone patu but he only got his wish if he'd been extra-brave in battle.

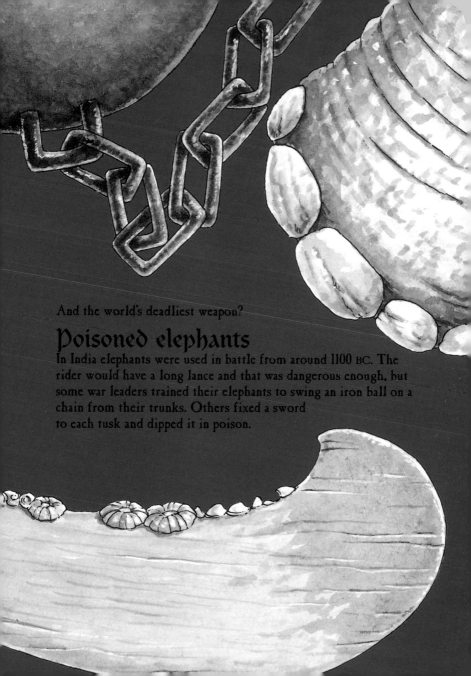

And the world's deadliest weapon?

Poisoned elephants

In India elephants were used in battle from around 1100 BC. The rider would have a long lance and that was dangerous enough, but some war leaders trained their elephants to swing an iron ball on a chain from their trunks. Others fixed a sword to each tusk and dipped it in poison.

Cut-throat combat

The idea of single combat is ancient. Two warriors meet and fight. The winner wins the battle for his side. One man dies ... but it saves hundreds of lives!

The most famous old tale is of David and Goliath, but there have been more bloody battles than that.

In 1583 two Irish chieftains decided to settle a quarrel by a fight to the death – mortal combat. This was the last such contest in Ireland and it would have made sensational reading if there had been newspapers in 1583! Just imagine it...

The Dublin Daily
3 May 1583

CONOR CUT TO THE COBBLES
From our ace sports reporter, Sean Short

This morning blood is still being washed from the cobbles of the castle courtyard here in Dublin. That's all that remains of the bloodiest combat of the century.

Crowds turned out yesterday to watch two feuding O'Connells settle their differences once and for all. In the red corner was Tadgh and in the blue was Conor. Each man wore just a shirt and a helmet. Each was armed with just a sword and shield.

Before the bitter battle began the furious fighters were searched for hidden weapons – but it's pretty difficult to hide a weapon when you're wearing just a shirt. They sat on small stools in opposite corners of the yard, snarling insults and threatening murderous mutilation to one another. Then the constable of the castle gave the trumpet signal and the two men rushed across the cobbles to do battle.

Some spectators were a bit disappointed that the battle was over quite quickly. Terrible Tadgh chopped Conor's legs and cut him twice. The loss of blood soon weakened the woeful warrior and Tadgh was able to snatch his enemy's sword, turn it round and batter at his head with the handle. Conor's helmet crashed on the cobbles and it was curtains.

By this time the crowd were screaming 'Kill! Kill! Kill!' So he killed. Tadgh sliced Conor's head off with his own sword then passed the head to his family.

Today Conor's family were on their knees praying for his soul, while Dublin Castle cleaners were on their knees scrubbing. 'It'll take days to clean this mess up,' Mrs Molly O'Mopp moaned.

That's the sort of popular sports event you don't see much of today.

Native Americans

Powerful men of the plains crushed by cavalry
Place: North America. Time: from pre-history to now

The Native Americans lived in tribes and were great hunters and warriors. Their way of life was harsh. They had some odd beliefs – like drinking the blood of a brave man would give you his courage. They could be cruel.

A French priest went to Canada to preach to the native Americans.

This Iroquois tribe letter is based on a true story.

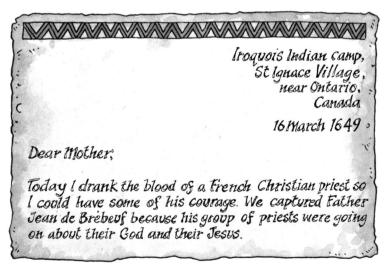

Iroquois Indian Camp,
St Ignace Village,
near Ontario,
Canada

16 March 1649

Dear Mother,

Today I drank the blood of a French Christian priest so I could have some of his courage. We captured Father Jean de Brébeuf because his group of priests were going on about their God and their Jesus.

We decided to torture those foolish ideas out of them. First we stripped him and bound him to a post; we tore out his fingernails and beat him with sticks. He just said, 'God will give me glory'. So we poured boiling water over his head and put a string of red-hot tomahawk heads round his neck.

We gave him a belt of wood and set fire to it. Still he didn't beg for mercy. He just kept telling us about his Jesus. To stop him we cut out his tongue and cut off his lips – we scalped him and still he lived. We cut off part of his leg and roasted it in front of him to eat it. As he was about to die an Iroquois cut out his heart and ate it. Maybe his Jesus God is a powerful God after all?

your loving son

The head of Jean de Brébeuf is still kept as a relic at the Hôtel-Dieu in Quebec.

But the native Americans had no answer to the guns of the American settlers:

1831 Native America Indians are getting in the way of settlers moving west. So the Indians are told to move even further west. They are kept on 'Reservations' and cannot hunt where they used to. So...

1876 Gold is discovered in the hills of Dakota and miners rush to the Indian land. The Indian warriors rebel and General Custer of the US Cavalry goes in to sort them out. Chief Crazy Horse, Chief Sitting Bull and their Sioux warriors meet him in battle. It is Custer who is killed.

1877 The mighty American army turns its full force on the Indians. Crazy Horse is penned in his reservation and Sitting Bull flees to Canada. It's the end for the free Native American Indians.

☠ **DID YOU KNOW…?** ☠

General William Tecumseh Sherman of the US Army had a simple little mind. In 1867 Sherman's simple mind had a simple answer to the Indians…

The more Indians we can kill this year, the less will have to be killed next year. The more I see of these Indians, the more sure I am they all have to be killed.

(The Indians didn't think much of him either.)

Two years later Sherman's simple friend General Sheridan said something just as vicious…

The only good Indian is a dead Indian!

The problem isn't that a couple of beanbag-brained generals said these things. The problem is that so many Americans agreed with them!

Woe for warriors

Warriors don't just make misery and bring pain to people. They also get themselves horrible hurt.

If you think being a warrior is wonderful then learn from these terrible tales of woe...

Soldier suffering

Those weapons could do dreadful damage, even when your enemy was wearing armour.

At the Battle of Poitiers the English defeated the French. The little English army fought desperately for seven hours and finally surrounded the French king, Jean II. The French knights fought and died to save him. The French historian Froissart described the battle as very, very bloody...

> Some of the French knights are cut in the belly and tread on their own guts. Others vomit their teeth. Some, still standing, have their arms cut off. The dying roll about in the blood of strangers, the fallen bodies groan.
>
> The ghosts, flying from the lifeless bodies, moan horribly. The bodies pile up around the waving battle-axe of king jean. His helmet is knocked off and he bleeds from wounds in the face.

'Surrender,' an English voice cries. 'Surrender or you are a dead man.'

A French rebel is the first of the English army to reach the king. 'Give yourself up and I will lead you safely to the English Prince.'

King Jean hands him his glove as a sign of surrender.

King Jean went as a prisoner to England until a vast ransom was paid. France was left without a king and many parts were 'ruled' by gangs of robbers for almost ten years.

Cool doc

English doctor William Harvey (born 1578) described what happened to Sir Adrian Scrope when he was wounded at Edgehill in the English Civil War.

Sir Adrian Scrope was dangerously wounded, and left amongst the dead men. The local people stripped him, which helped to save his life. It was cold, clear weather, and a frost that night, which stopped his bleeding, and about midnight, or some hours after his hurt, he woke up. He was forced to pull a dead body over himself for warmth.

Massacre of Ma'arra

Knights from Europe fought in the Crusades in Palestine. They could be ruthless.

At Ma'arra, many of the knights were starving. They managed to break down the town's walls and massacred about 20,000 Saracen enemies, as they often did. But, this time, as they could not find enough food, they went further.

A commander wrote a report to the Pope …

> *A terrible famine struck the army in Ma'arra, and forced the men to feed themselves upon the bodies of the Saracens.*

Radulph of Caen, another Crusader, wrote:

> *In Ma'arra our troops boiled Saracen adults alive in cooking-pots; they stuck children on spits and ate them grilled.*

Deadly Dracula

The real Count Dracula (Vlad Tepes) ruled in Romania from 1456 till 1476. He was a horribly cruel warrior. One of his nastiest tricks was to take a group of prisoners of war. He would have three of them fried alive. The others were then forced to eat them.

Top docs

Warriors can get horribly wounded in battle. Many doctors tried out new cures on dying soldiers – if they worked the soldier lived; if they didn't work the soldier would have died anyway.

Ambroise Paré was one of the most famous.

Paris Doctors'
Monthly 1539

The top army doc, Ambroise Paré, has come up with a sensational new treatment for soldiers who lose arms and legs in battle. He makes new mechanical body bits for them!

Paré's fake hands have pen holders built into them and some of them have fingers that move with the help of little cogs, like a clock. This fabulous Frenchman will even fit you false teeth or a false eye!

Of course Ambroise has become famous for his treatment of battle wounds. Old surgeons used boiling oil to pour into gunshot wounds – Ambroise uses a mixture of egg yolk, rose oil and turpentine. 'Far less painful ... and it works better,' one victim said happily.

And when a soldier has an arm or leg amputated in battle, the wound used to be 'sealed' with red-hot irons. Ouch! But our caring Ambroise started tying the blood vessels to stop the bleeding.

With docs like Ambroise Paré around it's almost a pleasure to get shot for France.

DID YOU KNOW...?

In Europe in the Middle Ages doctors were pretty clueless. They would try to cure a broken leg by wrapping a dog's brain in a bandage over the wound.

Mad Maori

Rowdy rebels who had a fing about flags
Place: New Zealand. Time: 1700s

The British reached New Zealand in 1769 and faced the Maori warriors. They shot a few as they usually did. The Maoris had no guns to shoot back.

The Brit settlers used a common trick. They made peace with the natives then got them to sign over the land to Queen Victoria. The Brits gave the Maoris booze and guns – the Maoris gave the Brits New Zealand.

BOOZE AND GUNS IS THE GOING RATE FOR A COUNTRY THIS SIZE

OK!

Five hundred Maori chiefs agreed to the deal!

But one of the chiefs, Hone Heke Pokai, became upset when he didn't get the wealth he was promised. He led a rebellion.

He couldn't attack the British guns and he couldn't attack Queen Victoria but he COULD attack the sign of her power – the British Union flag that flew from Flagstaff Hill.

If a Brit officer had written a diary of 1844 and 1845 then some of the entries may have looked like this…

20 July 1844

Maori raid on Kororareka. Chief Heke attacked Kororareka to rescue a Maori girl who was living with the local British butcher. She didn't even want to be rescued, poor girl! She used to be one of Heke's servants and she always called Heke 'Pig's head'. No one was hurt in the raid – but oddly one of Heke's friends chopped down our flagpole!

felled flag

17 August 1844

Our new flagpole stood proudly on Flagstaff Hill – until this morning. Some Maoris sneaked up and chopped it down again! It's guarded by 170 soldiers sent from Australia. We can't let sneaky Heke get away with it! Victoria's flag shall fly!

sneaky →

9 September 1844

New flagpole chopped down a third time. This is beyond a joke! Britannia rules the waves, and Britons never, never, never shall have their flags flattened. Captain Fitzroy has a marvellous plan to nobble the natives. He is taking a huge old ship's mast – thick as a tree trunk! The Maoris can attack it, but it will take them so long to chop down we'll have the army there to stop them. The post is defended by a small fort. That's the end of horrible Heke's game!

He! He!

11 March 1845

Disaster! The flagpole is down! The men at the fort were digging ditches when Heke's men leapt on them and massacred them with their knives and coral-studded clubs. Maoris also attacked the town and set it on fire. The biggest explosion was in the gunpowder dump – not caused by the Maoris, but by a British workman with a careless spark from his pipe! I always thought smoking was bad for your health. We British retreated to the safety of a warship – six men who returned for their valuables were hacked down. Final score, 19 British settlers dead and 29 wounded.

...all for the sake of a flag.

Rotten revenge

Of course the Brits sent in the army to get revenge. The band played 'Rule Britannia' as they landed. The British soldiers had the help of the friendly Maoris plus some 'pakeha' Maoris – British men who had gone to live with the natives. Men like Jackie Marmon, an ex-convict, who said he had...

- slaughtered rival Maoris in battle and
- eaten them at cannibal feasts!

Jackie could have been lying about noshing on natives, but it was true that a dead British soldier was found with neat pieces of meat sliced off his legs. Perhaps Jackey's Maori friends did eat people from time to time.

The Brits only finally defeated Heke by luck. The Maoris had become Christians and thought Sunday was a day of peace. The Brits (who were also supposed to be Christians) attacked on a Sunday when the Maoris were praying. (Which was a bit of a cheat! A bit like taking a football penalty kick while the goalkeeper is blowing his nose.)

And that flagpole? Heke died of a disease in 1850, six years after he started flattening flagpoles – but while he lived that flagpole was never raised again. So who won? No one.

Who lost? As usual, everyone.

Awesome Aborigines

Warriors with blood on their boomerangs
Place: Australia. Time: 1800s

Not everyone WANTS to be a warrior. Some people think they HAVE to fight to keep their families safe.

In 1770 British Captain James Cook landed in Australia. He said…

The Aboriginal may appear to be the most wretched people on Earth but in fact they are happier than we are in Europe. They live in peace and the earth and sea give them all they need.

OOPS!

Not for much longer.

There were horrors on both sides…

1788 Two British rush cutters are murdered and their bodies butchered.

1796 An Aboriginal girl who goes to live with the settlers is taken into the woods and hacked to death.

1800 Governor King arrives and makes a new rule: settlers can fire on any 'native' they see.

1802 Pemulwuy is one of the first Aborigines to fight back. He is shot. His head is cut off and sent to England.

1832 The British Army is made stronger to keep control of the convicts. They will soon be fighting the Aborigines.

1838 The Kamilaroi people of northern New South Wales are fierce warriors who upset the soldiers. It leads to the Massacre of the Aborigines at Slaughterhouse Creek.

1850s The Kamilaroi are finally defeated by Aborigine Police forces working for the British.

DID YOU KNOW…?

Twenty-eight unarmed Aborigines were killed at Slaughterhouse Creek, the youngest a baby boy aged three. A witness said…

The killers chased them like chickens round the pen, hacking off their heads as they ran.

Aboriginal warriors had duels just like warriors in Europe. Duels with rules. A British writer described them:

Their way of fighting is most cruel. In the case of a quarrel between two men, they stand about 20 paces apart, and each throws his spears at the other's thighs.

After a few turns they close in, and each man offers first his left thigh to the other to be stabbed with the larger spear.

This they continue in turns, and the one who falls first is the beaten. The victims are sometimes crippled for a few weeks and suffer greatly.

Charcoal is rubbed over the wounds to keep the flies off. In these 'camp fights' it is the law to avoid spearing each other above the thigh.

Neat names

Some warriors have had strange names. Can you match the name to its meaning?

Name	Means
1 Atahuallpa	A. Perfect ruler
2 Shaka	B. Head of an Ox
3 Malcolm Canmore	C. Gut ache
4 Genghis Khan	D. Man who shakes the earth
5 Tamerlane	E. Tough Ruler
6 Hardrada	F. Big head
7 Bucephalus[2]	G. Happy chicken
8 Pachacuti	H. Limping blacksmith

2 OK – so Bucephalus was a horse … but braver than some wet and wimpy warriors! So we'll put him in this list and see if you can work out what his name means.

Beastly Boxers

Freedom fighters aiming for foreign fools in their fists
Place: China. Time: founded 1890s

Empress Cixi of China wanted to get rid of the foreign people in her country. Traders from Europe were making themselves rich and leaving the Chinese very poor.

She got help from a secret society, known as the Fists of Righteous Harmony … the foreigners called them 'Boxers' because of the way they fought.

The Boxers also believed…

• that they had a prayer that gave them magical power
• that foreign bullets could not harm them
• that millions of 'spirit soldiers' would rise from the dead and join their fight

They wrote on their banners…

SUPPORT CHINA— KILL A FOREIGNER!

SNAPPY SLOGAN

ANY foreigner would do. They beat Christians and burned their homes. They attacked railways and the things foreigners had brought to China such as telegraph poles.

But when the Boxers attacked they were met by machine guns and cannon. They were blown to pieces.

The Empress dressed as a peasant and escaped in a cart. End of rebellion. End of Boxer warriors.

Sticky ends

Some warriors came to a very nasty end. Here are some who died horribly ... but don't feel too sorry for them because they probably deserved it.

Atahuallpa (1502–33)

Life: the last great chief of the Inca people in Peru.

• When his half-brother Huascar was emperor, Atahuallpa sent 'servants' to worship Huascar. In fact the servants were his best warriors. They massacred the palace guards and Atahuallpa became emperor. Nasty.

• Atahuallpa killed half-brother Huascar's guards cruelly. He ordered:

> I WANT THEM SACRIFICED! I WANT THEM HANGED, OR THROWN IN A LAKE WITH STONES AROUND THEIR NECKS OR THROWN FROM A CLIFF... AND YOU CAN LET *HUASCAR* WATCH THE FUN!

The women and children of the royal family had to go next. Two HUNDRED of them. They were starved and then hung by the neck or the waist and left to die. (A Spanish writer said they were hanged 'in ways too disgusting to mention' ... so we won't mention them.)

- This was still not enough for Awful Atah. The servants and water-carriers, the gardeners and cooks were massacred. In some cities just one man remained for every ten women.
- Now there were not enough soldiers left to attack him! Great! But there weren't enough soldiers left to fight the conquistadors either...

Sticky end:
- The Spanish Conquistadors arrived in 1532 with horses and cannon that the Incas couldn't fight.
- The Spanish set up an ambush in a square at Caxamarca city. Atahuallpa walked into the trap and was captured.
- Atahuallpa paid a huge ransom of gold and silver to the Conquistador leader Francisco Pizarro.
- Once he got the money Pizarro decided to execute Atahuallpa anyway ... which is a bit of a cheat.
- Atahuallpa did not want to be executed by burning – it would ruin his life as a 'god'. On 29 August 1533 he was tied to a post and strangled.

Francisco Pizarro (1475–1541)

OINK!

Life: The man who killed Emperor Atahuallpa in Peru.
- Pizarro was the son of a soldier and started life as a pig boy[3]. It is said he was cared for by a sow!
- With a small Spanish army he crossed the Atlantic and captured Peru in the search for gold.
- Pizarro could be very sneaky. He set a trap for his Inca enemies. When a huge army of Incas was in the city square his hidden cannon opened fire. The Incas had nowhere to run.

3 No, I don't mean he was half-pig and half-boy. I mean he was a boy who looked after pigs.

- Final score: Inca 7,000 dead, Spanish 0.
- Pizarro fought the natives and was happy to torture then burn their chiefs so he could steal their gold. That is what they would do to him if they had the chance, he said.
- Pizarro was even harsh on his own men. He forced them to march on when they were tired and starving. Sometimes they ate jungle lizards and monkeys, their own horses or their dogs. Could you eat meat from mutts?

Sticky end:
- Fran had a general called Diego de Almagro who was a bit jealous of him. He sent Almagro off to Chile to conquer it but Almagro messed it up.
- Almagro returned in 1536 and wanted a share of Pizarro's land in Peru. He fought against Pizarro's brothers to get it but was captured.
- Pizarro had Almagro executed – strangled just like Atahuallpa, then his head was sliced off just to make sure.
- Almagro's son and his Spanish friends set off looking for revenge. Fran had built himself a palace in Lima and that's where they got him. But he went down fighting. He killed two of his attackers and then they came up with a wonderful plan…

• Pizarro died a Christian. He dipped a finger in the blood from his throat and made the sign of a cross on the floor. He kissed the bloody cross ... then the last blows rained down on him. Plenty of people went to the funeral but no one cried.

• Did he deserve to be murdered? Well, the Incas had good reason to kill him ... but they didn't. His old Spanish friends killed him. Which, the dead dogs would say, is a bit ruff ... ruff.

☠☠ **DID YOU KNOW...?** ☠☠

The mummy of Pizarro was on show in Lima Cathedral for hundreds of years. Then in 1979 a skeleton was found under the floor with a label saying...

These are the bones of Don Francisco Pizarro, who discovered and won Peru [4]

The skeleton had lots of sword cuts. The mummy had NO sword cuts. So the REAL Pizarro was the skeleton, not the mummy. Who was the mummy? Probably some priest.

4 All right, the label was in Spanish so it didn't exactly say, 'These are the bones' and so on. But if we'd written it in Spanish you would complain, wouldn't you?

William the Conqueror (1028–87)

Life: William was the ruthless ruler of the Normans.

• Bill the Conk did not believe in the old saying 'Forgive and forget'. Shortly after he was crowned King of England there was a rebellion in the North of England where hundreds of his Normans were killed. A twelfth century history said:

> *William fell on the English in the North like a lion on its prey. He ordered that their houses, food, tools and belongings should be burnt and large herds of their cattle should be butchered. Thousands of children, old people, young men and women died of starvation.*

• William was tough ... but he was also touchy. He hated it when people reminded him his grandad was just a poor leather-worker. In 1047 he attacked the town of Alençon. The silly citizens decided to make fun of William's weakness. They hung out leather skins and cried...

> *Leather! Leather for the leather-worker's grandson!*

William waited and took a rotten revenge. He caught 32 of the top men from Alençon. First he marched them in front of the walls as the citizens watched ... and then he lopped off their hands and feet. He still wasn't finished. Sixty-four hands and sixty-four feet were flung over the city walls.

Sticky End:

• Fate plays strange tricks. The French King made some nasty remarks about William being too fat. 'I'll set the whole of France ablaze!' Big Bill threatened.

He started by setting fire to the castle at Mantes. But, as the fire burned, sparks flew in the air. Billy's horse stepped on a hot cinder and stumbled.

Bill fell forward on to the point of his saddle and did himself a nasty injury – probably burst his bladder. He died in agony.

• Bill was a pretty big bloke. That was just one of the problems that turned his funeral into a disaster ... or a farce:

1 His body went mouldy quickly.

2 Two of the undertakers caught a fever from the corpse and died.

3 As he was carried to his monastery tomb a fire broke out.

4 The mourners put the coffin down and went to fight the fire.

5 A man interrupted the funeral shouting that William had stolen the monastery land and had no right to be buried there. (The man was given money to shut him up!)

6 A stone tomb was made for him after his death. But he was large – and his body swelled a lot as it rotted so he was too big to fit in the tomb. As the body was forced in, bits dropped off it!

7 The smell was so bad the priests rushed through the funeral service ... then ran!

William Wallace (1270–1305)

Life: When Edward I of England tried to crush Scotland it was Wallace who led the rebellion against him. He defeated the English at Stirling Bridge.

• Wallace never had the support of all the great Scottish lords because he was not from a great family himself. In fact some of those lords wanted peace with England.

• There was an English story about Wallace's defeat of Hugh Cressingham in the Battle of Stirling Bridge. The story is that the Scots leader stripped the skin off Cressingham and made it into a belt for his sword. Other bits of skin were turned into girths for the Scottish horses or sent around Scotland to boast of the victory.

Sticky end:

• Wallace was betrayed. A Scots traitor called Monteith told him the Scottish authorities wanted him to promise peace. The giant Wallace allowed himself to be bound and handed over.

• The Scottish authorities handed him straight over to the avenging English king Edward I.

• Edward gave Wallace a sort of trial and sentenced him to die horribly.

1 He was strapped to a gate, naked and head down.

2 Then he was pulled by a horse for two miles to the gallows.

3 Even though his head was dragged over the ground he was still conscious when he was hung by the neck.

4 Before he was strangled he was cut down and his belly cut open.

5 His heart and bowels were ripped out and burned

6 The arms and legs were cut off the body and sent to decorate castles in England and Scotland as a warning to rebels.

7 The head was hung from the tower of London Bridge.

Shaka (1787–1828)

Life: Zulu leader who fought anyone and everyone in southern Africa.

• Shaka and his mother were sent away from the Zulu nation. Life was hard. They spent some time living in a cave, and Shaka grew up tough. Other boys picked on him, poor lad, because his naughty bits weren't very large.

• He grew to be a big youth (though his naughty bits stayed a bit on the small side) and returned to the Zulus to lead them – so the first thing he had to do was kill the chief … his own father.

• Shaka was a great warrior chief, but he was afraid a son would grow up to kill him. We can guess why he was worried about that! He had 1,200 wives but didn't want to be a father – so if one of his wives had a baby he murdered her! His 1,200 mothers-in-law must have been annoyed.

• Shaka punished any cowardly soldier with death. He also had them executed if they forgot to bring their spear to practice! (Imagine if there was death every time someone forgot their towel for school swimming lessons!) Shaka's soldiers were not allowed to have girlfriends either. The punishment? Death, of course.

• Between 1815 and 1828, Shaka destroyed all the tribes in southern Africa that were opposed to him. This jolly time became known as Mfecane … or 'The Terror'. He probably caused the deaths of a MILLION people – that is totally terrific terror.

Shaka seemed to enjoy being cruel. After he killed someone he had a little catchphrase you may like to copy. He shouted…

When Shaka's mother died he slaughtered thousands of PEOPLE. Shaka said,

It's reckoned 7,000 people were killed because Shaka's mother died!

Sticky end:

• Shaka's people had almost starved to death and he wasn't a popular lad any longer. Plots were plotted. But Shaka trusted his half-brothers, Dingaan and Mhlangane, and met them for a chat.

'We've come to kill you,' they said.

Shaka shook. The great chief grovelled. 'Please don't hurt me!'

---

5 You don't need me to tell you what that means! You do? Oh, all right then. It means, 'I have eaten!'

But they turned on him and started to hack him to death. As he fell he said some great last words…

Brothers! What have I done?

That's what you call a really good question. Sadly he didn't live long enough to hear the answer.

Mighty Shaka's body was thrown in an empty grain pot. (Corny, but true.) It was then filled with stones.

Pyrrhus of Epirus (319–272 BC)

WHOO-HOO! NO MORE SCHOOL!

Life: At the age of 12, Pyrrhus became King of Epirus (part of Greece and Albania).

• He was a great warrior and almost conquered Rome. The trouble was he never finished off a war before he was away starting a new one.

• Pyrrhus was attacked by an army of Mamertines – a fierce people from Sicily. In this fight Pyrrhus was wounded in the head by a sword, and was treated by a doctor.

• The biggest and best-armoured Mamertine rode into the Greek camp. He cried for Pyrrhus to come out and fight.

• Pyrrhus broke free of his doctors and his guards, pushed

through his men, and with one mighty stroke of his sword cut the giant in half from head to foot.

Sticky end:

• King Pyrrhus met a pathetic end in his battle to defeat the Romans. In 272 BC he was fighting at the siege of Argos when a peasant with a pike hurt him.

• The peasant didn't hurt the King very much, you understand, but Pyrrhus was furious and turned to smash the pike man with his sword.

Poor Pyrrhus reckoned without the women of Argos. They had climbed up to the rooftops to watch the battle. They must have been like proud parents watching a school football match. You know, the sort who stand on the touchline and shout things like, 'Get stuck in, our Timothy!' And, 'Come on, ref – get your eyes tested!'

Anyway, who should be watching Pyrrhus attacking the pike man peasant? The peasant's mum.

'Hey! That's my little boy you're trying to kill, you big bully!' she cried. The woman tore a tile off the roof and flung it at Pyrrhus.

The woman was either an Olympic-standard discus thrower, or very, very lucky. The tile cracked Pyrrhus on the back of the neck, just below the helmet. His neck was broken and he dropped dead from his horse.

An enemy lopped off his head to make sure.

Richard 1 of England (1157–99)

Life: Richard was known as the Lionheart. He spent most of his life fighting in the Crusades.

• Richard the Lionheart was chasing an enemy when the enemy turned to fight. The knight that faced Richard was the great champion William Marshal. Ooops! Richard realized that he'd forgotten to put his armour on. He cried…

The sporting Marshal did not want to kill an unarmed man ... so he killed Richard's horse instead!

> WALK HOME RICHARD THE CHICKENHEART

What had dead Dobbin done to deserve it? Sometimes it was horrible being a warrior's horse ... as you have already seen.

Sticky end:

• Richard I was riding around a French castle he was planning to capture. Bertram de Gurdin was one of the defenders. Weapons were so short that Bertram was using a frying pan for a shield! When Bert saw Richard riding below the castle walls he raised his crossbow and fired a bolt. The bolt hit the English King close to his neck

> WHAT'S WRONG WITH HAVING A BOLT IN THE NECK?

Richard was taken back to his camp where General Marchades dug around in the wound trying to get the head of the bolt out. He probably succeeded in getting lots of infection into the wound.

Richard grew ill, but his army went on to capture the castle. Bertram was brought before the dying King. Richard croaked weakly…

• Merchades had Bertram skinned alive and then hanged.

• Richard's guts were buried at the foot of the castle tower, his heart was buried at Rouen, while the rest of his body was buried next to his father at an abbey near Chinon in France.

> ✺ **DID YOU KNOW…?** ✺
>
> One evening Richard enjoyed a specially spicy and spiteful dish. It was said that he had the head of a Saracen enemy cut off and curried. He ate it.

8 Nadir Shah (1688-1747)

Life: Nadir made himself king of Persia in 1736.

• Nasty Nadir wanted huge armies so he could go around bashing his neighbours. But armies cost money and the money came from taxes on the people. Anyone who could not pay was executed.

• Nadir thought his own son, Reza Quli Mirza, was plotting against him.

Did Nadir give him a slap round the ear and tell him to behave? No.

Did he lock him in his room till he said 'Sorry'? No.
He had him blinded.

But some of his lords knew what Nadir had done – so Nadir had the lords executed to keep them quiet.

• Nadir enjoyed going on journeys round his country. But wherever he stopped to rest he had people tortured and put to death.

• Nasty Nadir had towers built from the skulls of his victims.

Sticky end:

• In March 1747 Nadir crossed the pitiless Dasht-i-Lut desert, where many of his men died from hunger and thirst.

• A group of his own tribe did not want to be next. As one chief said…

We decided to have him for breakfast before he had us for supper.

They attacked him in his sleep. He still managed to kill two attackers before they lopped off his head.

Nadir lost his nut.

Epilogue

What makes a warrior?

Greed
Alaric the Goth attacked Rome because his wife wanted the Roman jewels.

Religion
The Crusaders killed to make the world Christian.

Hunger
The Vikings sailed from the cold thin soil to find better farms.

Pride
The Spartans wanted to be the greatest Greeks.

Hatred
Dracula wanted to see his enemies suffer.

Defence
Joan of Arc wanted to save her people from the invading English.

Warriors have battled for many of these reasons and more.
You can understand why many of them felt they had to fight.

It's hard to understand why so many of them seemed to ENJOY making their enemies suffer before they died. Why they loved giving pain and misery. Why they tortured and killed women and children as well as enemy warriors.

Samurai and conquistadors, knights and ninjas are gone now. But new warriors have taken their places.

Will the world ever be free of warriors?

Interesting Index

Hang on! This isn't one of your boring old indexes. This is a horrible index. It's the only index in the world where you will find 'burst bladder', 'underpants', 'mouldy bodies' and all the other things you really HAVE to know if you want to be a horrible historian. Read it and creep.

Grab yourself a copy of this horrible handy hanbook - it's everything you need to know about pirates, all the gore and more!

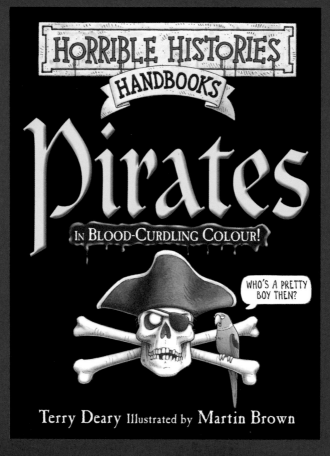

ISBN: 0 439 95578 5 £5.99

Want to know all the knasty bits about knights? Pick up this horribly handy handbook for the terrible truth about the cold-blooded killers.

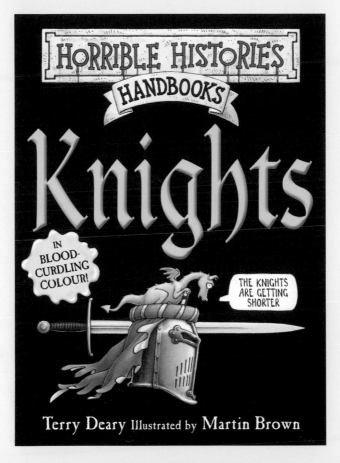

ISBN: 0 439 95577 7 £5.99

For a terrifying treat this Hallowe'en don't
miss the horrible history of witches – full of
foul facts and nasty bits.
Coming September 2007

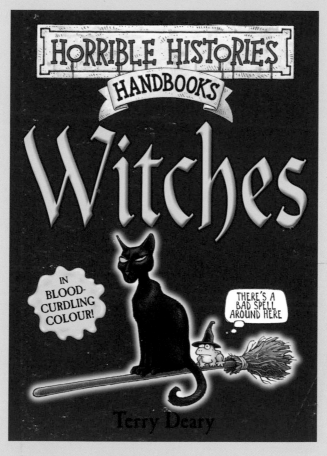

ISBN: 0 439 94986 6 £5.99